the facts about
SOLIDS, LIQUIDS,
and GASES

Rebecca Hunter

A+

First published in 2003 by Franklin Watts
Franklin Watts, 96 Leonard Street, London EC2A 4XD

Franklin Watts Australia
45–51 Huntley Street, Alexandria, NSW 2015
This edition published under license from Franklin Watts. All
rights reserved.

Editor: Rebecca Hunter; Design: Keith Williams; Consultant:
Jeremy Bloomfield; Illustrations: Peter Bull: pages 24–25;
Keith Williams: page 26

Published in the United States by Smart Apple Media
1980 Lookout Drive, North Mankato, Minnesota 56003

Library of Congress Cataloging-in-Publication Data

Hunter, Rebecca (Rebecca K. de C.)
The facts about solids, liquids, and gases / by Rebecca
Hunter. p. cm. — (Science the facts)
Includes index.
Contents: Looking at materials—Solids, liquids, and gases—
Describing solids, liquids and gases—Reversible changes—
Irreversible changes—Making mixtures—Solutions and
suspensions—Separating mixtures—Filtration, evaporation
and distillation—Water—The water cycle—Gases around
us—Materials in use.
ISBN 1-58340-450-3
1. Matter—Properties—Juvenile literature. [1. Matter—
Properties.] I Title: Solids, liquids, and gases. II. Title. III.
Series.

QC73.36.H84 2003
530.4 — dc22   2003060723

9 8 7 6 5 4 3 2 1

Photographs:
Bruce Coleman Collection: page 25 (Janos Jurka), page 28
top (Tore Hagman); Corbis Images: page 7, page 10 left,
page 12, page 16, page 17, page 27, page 28 bottom;
Chris Fairclough: page 8, page 17 bottom, page 18,
page 19, page 29 both; Discovery Picture Library: page
6 both, page 9 top, page 10 right, page 13 top, page
22; Oxford Scientific Films: page 4 (William Gray), page
5 bottom (Lou E Lauber), page 9 bottom (Laurence Gould),
page 11 (Hjalmar Bardarson), page 13 bottom (Colin
Monteath), page 26 (Bruce Herrod); Rebecca Hunter:
page 5 top, page 14; Science Picture Library: cover
(Bernhard Edmaier), page 15 (Charles D Winters), page
20 (Pascal Goetgheluck), page 21 (Martin Bond), page 23
(Mehan Kulyk).

the facts about

SOLIDS, LIQUIDS, and GASES

Contents

Words in **bold** appear in the glossary on page 30.

Looking at materials

The word "materials" describes what things are made of. Everything in the world is made of some sort of material.

Look around you now and see just how many types of materials there are. You are probably in a building which is made of bricks, stone, or wood. The windows are made of glass, and the floor might be made of wood or concrete.

◄ This girl is wearing cotton clothing. Her shoes are probably made of nylon with rubber soles.

Look at what you are wearing. You might have nylon or leather shoes with rubber soles. Your clothing might be made of cotton fabric or polyester. There are hundreds of different types of materials, and they come from different sources.

Natural materials

Natural materials are things that occur naturally on Earth. Many of these are found underground. Building materials such as stone, slate, gravel, and sand are all found on or beneath Earth's surface, as are metals, coal, and oil. They have to be mined or drilled to get them out.

Some natural materials come from living things. Trees provide several types of materials. In addition to wood, which we use in many different ways, rubber comes from the sap of a rubber tree, and cork is the bark of the cork tree.

Animals also provide us with materials. Wool, silk, and leather are all animal products.

◄ Sheep provide us with two useful natural materials: meat for food and wool for clothing.

Synthetic materials

Synthetic materials are those that have been made by people—they do not occur naturally. Plastics are made from chemicals in factories. The chemicals come mostly from oil. Polythene, nylon, polystyrene, and PVC are some of the many types of plastics. Fiberglass is a very strong synthetic material that is made by strengthening plastic with fibers of glass.

Changing materials

Sometimes we change natural materials into other materials. Glass is made by heating together sand, limestone, and a chemical called sodium carbonate. Building bricks and china crockery are made from clay, and paper is made from wood.

To understand why materials are useful to us, we need to look at their **properties**.

▼ This tree is being cut down for **timber**. We use wood products in many different ways.

key facts

- All things are made of materials.
- Materials can be natural or synthetic.
- Materials can be changed into other materials.

Solids, liquids, and gases

All materials, which scientists call matter, can be put into one of three groups: solids, liquids, or gases. These are called the three **states** of matter.

Solids

Anything that can be picked up and held in the hand is a solid. Solids have a particular shape that is not easy to change. Solids can be cut or shaped, but they do not flow easily. We are surrounded by solid things. The chair you are sitting on and the book you are reading are solids.

▼ These wax crayons are solids.

Liquids

Liquids are runny and always try to flow downward. Liquids do not have a particular shape like solids do. They always take the shape of the container they are in. If you have a bucket of water, the water takes the shape of the bucket. You could use the bucket to fill 20 glasses of water. The water would take the shape of the glasses. Or you could tip the bucket over and the water would make the shape of a big, flat puddle.

▲ Liquids take the shape of their container. This drink takes the shape of the glass and the straw.

Gases

We are surrounded by air that is made up of many gases. Gases have no shape at all and spread out to fill any container they are in. If you take a **helium** party balloon and make a hole in it, the helium will escape from the balloon and in a short while will have spread out all over the room.

Most gases are invisible, so it is quite difficult to see how they behave. One thing that can be done with gases that is hard to do with solids and liquids is to squeeze them. If **pressure** is put on a gas, it can be squeezed into a small space. A football is full of air that is under pressure inside a plastic ball.

▲ Balloons are used for festivities all over the world. A balloon is filled with gas (usually air or helium) under pressure.

key facts

- Solids have a definite shape.
- Liquids take the shape of their container.
- Gases have no shape and spread out to fill any space they are in.

Describing solids, liquids, and gases

All solids, liquids, and gases have properties or qualities that make them unique. Some of these are very useful to us.

When we need a certain material to do a particular job, we choose the one that has the most suitable properties. It is important to choose carefully. Paper is not ideal for building a house, and a teapot made of chocolate would not be much use for making tea!

Properties of solids

Solids can be hard or soft. They can be **rigid** like metal scaffolding poles or **flexible** like rubber tires. Some solids are **absorbent**, which means they soak up liquids; others are waterproof and **repel** liquids. If a barrier that will keep out the weather but let in the light is needed, then glass, which is a **transparent** solid, is used. Something that is cloudy, or not see-through, is a **translucent** material.

You can do it...

Many words describe solids. Can you think of a different solid for each of these properties: strong, heavy, light, stretchy, waterproof, transparent, brittle, pliable, powdery?

▼ Butter is a solid that has a definite shape, but it can be cut and spread easily.

Liquids

Liquids are fluids, which means they flow. Some flow more easily than others. Syrup and honey are liquids that flow slowly. Water flows much more quickly. Oil is a smoothly-flowing liquid. It is very useful as a **lubricant** between metal parts in machines. It stops them from rubbing against each other and wearing out.

Useful gases

Some gases are very useful to us. We need the gas oxygen to breathe; without it there would be no life on Earth. Many other gases also have useful properties. Carbon dioxide is a gas that is put in drinks to make them fizzy. Natural gas is used as a fuel in homes and to generate electricity.

◀ Honey is a liquid which flows quite slowly.

key facts

○ Solids have many useful properties.

○ Liquids are called fluids, which means they flow.

○ Oxygen is a gas that we need to live.

◀ Divers take tanks of oxygen underwater with them. A dial shows them how much oxygen is left.

Reversible changes

Some materials change state when their temperature is changed.

Many materials can turn from solids into liquids, or from liquids into gases. They can also change from gases into liquids and from liquids into solids. Because the materials 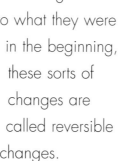 can be changed back to what they were in the beginning, these sorts of changes are called reversible changes.

Melting and evaporation

When some solids are heated, they melt and turn into a liquid. This can be seen when people are cooking; butter or chocolate may be melted to mix into other ingredients.

▲ This is melted chocolate. It is being poured out to cool and will harden to a solid, flat, circular shape.

Materials melt at different temperatures, called the melting point. The melting point of ice is 32 °F (0 °C). At this temperature, solid ice turns into liquid water. To make steel, iron is heated to a temperature of 3,452 °F (1,900 °C).

When a liquid is heated, it eventually boils and turns into a gas. This is called **evaporation**. The boiling point of water, when it evaporates into a gas called **water vapor**, is 212 °F (100 °C).

Freezing and condensing

The processes of melting and evaporating are reversible. When melted substances cool down, they turn back into solids. Water freezes and becomes ice. When gases are cooled, they turn back into liquids. You can see this happening in a bathroom or kitchen. When hot steam meets cold tiles or glass, little droplets of water appear on the cold surfaces. This process is called **condensation**.

These changes of freezing, melting, evaporating, and condensing are called physical changes. Ice looks and feels different from water, but it is still made of the same substance; the chemical make-up of the material has not changed.

▲ When molten **lava** pours out of a volcano it is a very hot liquid. Eventually it cools and becomes a solid dark-colored rock.

key facts

- Materials can change their state.
- Changing state is a physical change.
- Physical changes are reversible.

Irreversible changes

When a chemical change takes place, the materials break down completely. They change into something else. This is a permanent change; it cannot be reversed.

Burning

Burning is an irreversible change. When something is burned the materials that are burned change completely. If paper and wood are burned on a bonfire, all that will be left is ash. There is no way to turn this ash back into wood.

▼ A fire sweeps through trees and bushes beside a lake. Burning is an irreversible change; this undergrowth will be reduced to ash.

Rusting

When iron or steel are exposed to the air they will rust. This is a chemical **reaction**. The metals react with water and oxygen in the air to form iron oxide, or rust. Rust works its way through the metal, making it weaker. Ships, for example, which spend all their time in the water, are permanently at risk from rust. They must be covered with protective paint to stop the rust from damaging them.

Useful chemical changes

Some chemical changes are very useful to us. Cooking is an example of this. Eggs, flour, and sugar can be mixed together to make a cake. Once the cake is baked, the ingredients have gone through a chemical reaction and become something else. It is impossible to get the raw ingredients back again.

Burning fuel is a very important chemical change. For thousands of years people have burned wood and coal to keep warm and to cook with. We still burn many forms of fuel to provide energy. Much of our electricity is produced by burning coal, oil, or natural gas. Oil is also used to produce other fuels such as the gasoline and diesel used in airplanes and cars.

▼ A pile of rusty cars in a junk yard. Cars are made of steel, which rusts when exposed to water and oxygen.

▲ The food we eat is a form of fuel. The food undergoes a chemical change similar to burning inside our bodies, providing us with the energy we need to move around, work, and play.

key facts

- In a chemical change, the change is permanent and cannot be reversed.

- Burning, rusting, and cooking are examples of irreversible changes.

Making mixtures

If one or more materials are mixed together, a mixture is made. Solids, liquids, and gases can mix together in different ways.

Mixing solids

Some food products are made up of a mixture of ingredients. Some granola, for example, is made from oats, wheat flakes, milk powder, dried fruit, and nuts. Without any liquid, the solids remain separate.

▲ Concrete is made by mixing together sand, cement, and stones. When water is added to the dry ingredients, a chemical reaction happens that causes the concrete to set hard.

Sometimes we mix a solid and a liquid together to form a mixture called a **paste**. Poster paints are made by mixing colored powder (a solid) with water (a liquid). When the paint is used, the water evaporates, leaving the powder behind on the paper.

Mixing liquids

Many liquids are actually a mixture of two or more liquids. For example, tomato ketchup is a mixture of three liquids: tomato sauce, vinegar, and glucose syrup.

Water is added to another liquid to **dilute** it. This is what happens when orange juice is made. A lot of water is added to a small amount of **concentrated** juice.

Some liquids will not mix together. This often happens when trying to mix an oily liquid with a watery one. When a salad dressing is made, for example, oil is mixed with vinegar. These two liquids do not mix together well. The bottle must be shaken hard before the dressing can be used, so that the liquids are temporarily mixed up.

► Drinks are made fizzy by the addition of the gas carbon dioxide.

You can do it...

Make your own fizzy drink! Mix together 4 teaspoons of citric acid, 2 tablespoons of icing sugar and 2 tablespoons of bicarbonate of soda. Mix up a jug of orange juice. Add some of the powder and stir it well. Taste the drink. Keep adding the mixture a little at a time until you have a delicious-tasting fizzy drink.

Gases

It is difficult to imagine gases mixing with anything—but they do. When you drink a fizzy drink, such as soda pop, you are drinking a liquid with a gas **dissolved** in it. The bubbles are made of the gas carbon dioxide.

Gases can also mix with solids. The smoke that comes off a fire is actually a mixture of air and small particles of ash; the ash is what you are actually seeing when you see smoke.

key facts

- Solids, liquids, and gases can be mixed together.

- Liquids and solids can mix to form a paste.

- Fizzy liquids have a gas dissolved in them.

Solutions and suspensions

A solution is a liquid that has one or more other things dissolved in it. Some things that dissolve in a liquid seem to disappear, but in fact they have mixed together with the liquid.

Seawater, for example, looks clear but actually contains many things such as salt and **minerals** dissolved in it. It's easy to tell that there is salt in seawater by the rock pools at low tide. Crystals of salt that have been left behind after the water has evaporated can often be seen.

▼ The Great Salt Lake in Utah has a large amount of salt dissolved in it. When the water evaporates from the plants and rocks on the lake's shore, a thick coat of salt is left behind.

Making solutions

Solutions are made by dissolving a solid into a liquid. One example is sugar added to a cup of tea or coffee. The sugar is "soluble" in water. Sugar dissolves more quickly in hot water, and stirring also helps speed up the process. There is a limit to how much of a solid can be dissolved in an amount of water. When this limit is reached, no more of the solid will dissolve; some will stay undissolved. The amount of solid that can be added before this happens varies for different solids.

Take two identical glasses of warm water. Add a teaspoon of salt to one and a teaspoon of sugar to the other. Stir well so that they dissolve. Keep adding salt to one and sugar to the other until no more will dissolve. Did the same amount of solid dissolve in each glass?

▲ Water from the Yellow River in China is full of mud and silt in suspension. They give the river both its color and its name.

Suspensions

Some materials do not dissolve in water. They may float on top of the water or they may sink to the bottom. Sometimes pieces may stay floating within the liquid; these pieces are suspended, and we say the mixture is a **suspension**.

If you take a handful of soil and put it in a jar of water and mix it, you will see all three of these things happen. Bits of wood and leaf will float, stones and sand will sink, and tiny pieces of soil will stay in suspension. If you look closely, you can actually see the tiny particles suspended in the water.

key facts

 Some solids dissolve in liquids to make a solution.

Things that dissolve in liquids are soluble.

A suspension is a mixture of tiny particles suspended in a liquid.

Separating mixtures

Separating mixed-up materials can be very necessary when we need only one part of the mixture. There are several ways to separate mixtures.

Solids from solids

The easiest way to separate solids from solids is to sift them. This separates big bits from smaller bits. Good cooks always sift their flour before using it in baking. This removes any lumps. Outdoors, gardeners may need to sift the soil to remove stones and other large objects.

Sometimes one material can be used to help separate mixtures. For example, there are two ways in which a mixture of **iron filings** and talcum powder could be separated. Moving a **magnet** over the mixture would cause all the iron filings to jump out and cling to it. If the mixture were poured into water, the iron filings would sink and the talcum powder would float on the surface.

► Sifting soil is a good way to remove stones, leaves, and twigs. Only the fine, useful soil gets through.

▼ This dirty water was left to stand still overnight. The next day the sediment had settled on the bottom of the jug and it was possible to pour off relatively clean water. This water could be filtered (*see page 20*) to clean it further.

You can do it...

Make a mixture of paper clips, rice, sugar, and talcum powder. Now see if you can separate all the substances. Clue: You will need to use water, a sieve, and a magnet. (Make sure you use them in the right order.)

Decanting

Decanting is one way of separating liquids from the solids suspended in them. It is particularly useful for cleaning water. Dirty water is left to stand still and the mud particles eventually settle on the bottom as sediment. The clean water can then be carefully poured off (or decanted). Many ancient civilizations used this method as the first stage in cleaning river water so that they could drink it.

key facts

◯ Sifting separates solids from other solids.

◯ Decanting separates suspended solids from liquids.

Filtration, evaporation, and distillation

Filtration, evaporation, and distillation are some other ways of separating solids and liquids.

Filtration is like sifting, only the solids are much smaller and so the sieve has to be much finer. A fine sieve is called a filter. One way to make coffee is to place ground coffee beans in a filter paper and pour hot water over them. Some of the coffee dissolves in the water and passes through the filter—this is what is drank. The solid coffee grounds are too large to pass through the filter and are left behind.

When water is **purified** for drinking it goes through several series of filters. First, it passes through a screen that removes objects such as twigs and trash. It then goes through sand and gravel filters that remove smaller particles. Finally, the water is treated to remove anything that might be harmful to us if we drank it.

◄ Coffee is made by separating the liquid coffee from the ground beans by filtration.

▼ These are filter beds at a sewage plant. The beds consist of fine gravel and sand and are used to filter solid particles from liquid sewage.

Evaporation

A solid that is soluble in water will be able to pass through a filter with the water. To get the solid back from a solution, the water must be heated. When the water evaporates, the solid will be left behind (*see page 16*). This process of removing a liquid by heat is called evaporation.

Distillation

To get the water back from a solution, a process called distillation is used. In distillation, the liquid is heated until the water evaporates. This water vapor is then passed through a tube that is being cooled by having cold water run over it. The water vapor in the tube condenses back into water and is collected for use.

key facts

- Filtration can separate solids from liquids.
- Evaporation removes liquids from soluble solids.
- Distillation removes water from liquids.

Water

Water is the most important substance on Earth. All plants and animals are largely made of water, and they all depend on water for life.

More than 70 percent of Earth's surface is covered by oceans and seas. Another 10 percent is covered by water in the form of ice. All living things are made mostly of water. About 60 percent of the human body is composed of water. Most fruits and vegetables are almost totally made of water.

Both plants and animals need to drink or take in water in order to survive. A human cannot live more than four days without water.

▲ Fruits are about 95 percent water.

Show how water expands when frozen. Take a small plastic tub with a lid. Fill it right up to the top with water and press on the lid. Leave it in the freezer overnight. When you take it out, you will find that the freezing water has expanded enough to push the lid off!

▶ This photograph of an ice cube on a hot surface shows the material water in all three of its states: as ice, water, and water vapor.

States of water

Water is unusual because it is the only material that can be found naturally in all three states. We are most familiar with it as a liquid in rivers and lakes, or coming out of taps in our houses. But the gas, water vapor, is constantly around us in the air. When the temperature drops below 32 °F (0 °C) water freezes, so in winter solid ice can be seen on puddles or as icicles forming as water drips off trees or buildings.

key facts

- More than 70 percent of Earth's surface is covered by water.
- Water is essential for life.
- Water exists on Earth naturally in all three states: as a solid, a liquid, and a gas.

The water cycle

The movement of water around the planet in the **atmosphere** (as rain) and through rivers, lakes, and oceans is called the water cycle.

There is never any new water on Earth. All the water that we see in rain, in rivers, in sinks and bathtubs, and in the sea, is being recycled all the time. The rain that falls today has fallen billions of times before and will fall billions of times again. This continuous recycling of water is known as the water cycle.

Water on Earth's surface is heated by the sun and evaporates as water vapor into the atmosphere. As it rises up into the air, it cools and condenses back into water again. Water droplets collect together to form clouds. They fall back to Earth's surface as rain, and so the water cycle continues.

The water cycle

3 Water droplets collect and form clouds.

2 As water vapor rises into the air, it cools and condenses back into water droplets.

1 Both the sun and the wind cause water in rivers, lakes, and seas to evaporate into the air as water vapor.

5 Water flows back into rivers and down to the sea.

4 Water falls back to Earth as rain, sleet, hail, or snow.

key facts

- Water is constantly being recycled on Earth.

- The sun and wind cause water to evaporate.

DOROTHY LYNAS

Gases around us

Most gases cannot be seen, smelled, or tasted, but they surround us all the time. Some are very important to us.

The atmosphere

The atmosphere is the layer of gases that surrounds Earth. The gases are a mixture which we call air. As with water, the atmosphere is essential to life on Earth. It is like a protective blanket around the world. It keeps us warm and protects us from the harmful rays of the sun. It also provides us with the gas oxygen that we and all animals need to breathe.

The atmosphere is mostly made up of nitrogen. Nitrogen is very important to all living things; it forms part of the **proteins** in every living **cell**.

1% Others
21% Oxygen
78% Nitrogen

▲ The atmosphere is made up of a mixture of gases. The main ones are nitrogen and oxygen.

Natural gas

Along with oil, natural gas was formed by prehistoric plants and animals that were buried under the sea millions of years ago. The gas they created, called methane, is very useful to us as a fuel. Huge drilling platforms sink deep wells into the sea bed to find the gas underneath. When the gas has been extracted, it is cooled and stored as a liquid. It may be piped into homes to be burned for heating and cooking, or it may be used in power plants to produce electricity.

Light gases

Some gases are lighter than air. This means that a balloon filled with them will float upward. The gas hydrogen was used to

▲ Drilling platforms like this are built at sea to bring oil and natural gas up from beneath the sea bed. The gas may be as deep as 3.7 miles (6 km) below the surface.

key facts

○ 78 percent of the atmosphere is made up of the gas nitrogen.

○ Natural gas, or methane, is found underground.

○ Some gases burn easily; others do not.

fill **airships** in the 1930s. Unfortunately, hydrogen burns very easily, and there were many horrifying airship explosions. Helium is also a light gas. Unlike hydrogen, it does not burn, making it much safer for use in modern balloons and airships.

▶ The *Hindenburg*, a German airship, was filled with hydrogen. In 1937, it exploded into flames, killing many people on board.

Materials in use

We have seen how the materials in our world can exist in three different states: as solids, liquids, and gases.

Physical changes

Extreme changes in temperature cause materials to change state. When heated, many solids will melt; liquids will evaporate into gases. A lowering of temperature causes gases to condense into liquids and liquids to change into solids.

Chemical changes

Changes that involve a chemical rather than a physical reaction are not reversible. Sometimes these changes are useful ones, such as cooking or baking. Others are less useful; when your house burns down, there is no way to reverse the chemical change in the materials of the house caused by the burning fire.

▲ This barrel has been floating in the sea for some time. The effects of water, salt, and oxygen in the air have caused a chemical reaction called rusting to occur.

▼ The metal iron can be melted at high temperatures and used to manufacture a much stronger metal called steel. Steel is used to make many things from cutlery to cars.

◄ When salt and water are mixed together in a saucepan, the salt dissolves in the water to make a salt solution.

Mixtures

Solids, liquids, and gases can be mixed together in many different ways. Solids can be mixed with solids to form new solids, or they can be mixed with liquids to form pastes or solutions. Gases can be mixed with liquids to make fizzy drinks, or they can mix with solid particles—such as when water vapor mixes with ash particles to form smoke or smog.

Separating mixtures

Sometimes mixtures of materials are no use to us unless they can be separated. The process that is used for separation depends on which part of the mixture is needed.

Solids can be separated from liquids by sifting or filtration. The solids are left in the sieve or filter, while the liquid is able to pass through. Solids can be separated from liquid solutions by letting the water evaporate. This is the way salt is obtained from seawater.

key facts

- Materials can exist in three states: solids, liquids, and gases.

- Materials can change state according to temperature.

- Changes in state are reversible changes.

- Chemical changes are irreversible changes.

- Materials can be mixed together to make different materials.

- Mixtures of materials often need to be separated to be useful.

Glossary

Absorbent Something that can take in water.

Airship A large balloon designed to carry passengers. It is filled with a gas such as helium that is lighter than air.

Atmosphere The layer of gases that surrounds Earth.

Cell The smallest unit of an organism that can exist on its own.

Concentrated When a large amount of something is contained in a small space.

Condensation When a gas changes to a liquid.

Decanting Separating a liquid from a solid by allowing the solid to settle and then pouring off the liquid.

Dilute To add more water.

Dissolve When a solid or gas mixes with a liquid to make a new solution.

Distillation A process in which a liquid is boiled and then condensed. It is used to separate one liquid from another.

Evaporate When a liquid changes to a gas.

Filtration A process in which a solid is removed from a liquid by passing the mixture through a filter.

Flexible Something that is bendy or elastic.

Helium A gas that is lighter than air and does not burn.

Iron filings Tiny shavings of iron.

Lava The liquid rock that comes out of a volcano.

Lubricant An oily substance used to reduce friction.

Magnet A material that is attracted to certain metals.

Minerals Naturally occurring substances such as metals and oil.

Paste A solid that is mixed with a small amount of liquid.

Pressure The amount of force pushing on something.

Properties The qualities of a certain material.

Protein A substance found in foods that the body uses for growth and repair.

Purify To make clean.

Reaction A change that alters the chemical properties of a substance.

Repel To push something away.

Rigid Something that is stiff, not flexible.

State Solid, liquid, or gas. A material can be in one of these three states.

Suspension A mixture of tiny particles of a solid in a liquid.

Timber Trees that have been cut down to use the wood.

Translucent Something that lets some light through but cannot be seen through clearly.

Transparent Something that can be seen through.

Water vapor Water in the form of a gas.

Further information

Books

Frankel Hauser, Jill. *Super Science Concoctions: 50 Mysterious Mixtures for Fabulous Fun.* Charlotte, Vermont: Williamson Publishing, 2003.

Hewitt, Sally. *Everyday Chemicals.* Brookfield, Conn.: Copper Beech Books, 2003.

Hunter, Rebecca. *Matter.* Portsmouth, New Hampshire: Heinemann Library, 2003.

Richards, Jon. *Chemicals.* London: Franklin Watts, 2002.

Web sites

Chem4Kids
A beginner's look into the states of matter, atoms, reactions, and other elements of chemistry.
http://www.chem4kids.com/index.html

BrainPOP: Matter and Molecules
Watch cartoons, do quizzes, and try experiments to learn about the building blocks of the universe, including mass and density, atoms, the pH scale, and water.
http://www.brainpop.com/science/matter/

Grade 3: Water
Learn all about water in its solid, liquid, and gas forms.
http://www.nyu.edu/pages/mathmol/textbook/3gradecover.html

Places to Visit

U.S.
American Museum of Natural History
New York City, New York
http://www.amnh.org

Field Museum of Natural History
Chicago, Illinois
http://www.fieldmuseum.org

Museum of Science and Industry
Chicago, Illinois
http://www.msichicago.org

Pacific Science Center
Seattle, Washington
http://www.pacsci.org

Science Museum of Minnesota
St. Paul, Minnesota
http://www.smm.org

Smithsonian Institution
Washington, DC
http://www.si.edu

Canada
Canada Science and Technology Museum
Ottawa, Ontario
http://www.sciencetech.technomuses.ca

Provincial Museum of Alberta
Edmonton, Alberta
http://www.pma.edmonton.ab.ca

Index